New Growth Press, Greensboro, NC 27401

Text Copyright © 2024 by Marty Machowski

Illustration Copyright © 2024 by Phil Schorr

Cover/Interior Design: Phil Schorr

ISBN 978-1-64507-415-1

Library of Congress Cataloging-in-Publication Data on file

Printed in Canada

31 30 29 28 27 26 25 24   2 3 4 5 6

PROMISES MADE
PROMISES KEPT

A FAMILY DEVOTIONAL
FOR CHRISTMAS

MARTY MACHOWSKI

ILLUSTRATED BY PHIL SCHORR

New Growth Press

CONTENTS

GOD DELIVERED HIS FIRST CHRISTMAS PROMISE VERY EARLY IN THE CREATION STORY—RIGHT AFTER ADAM AND EVE SINNED.

In the beginning, God created the heavens and the earth. Where there had been nothing, he created everything—all by his power. God made man, Adam, out of the dust of the earth and gave him breath. Then God created woman, Eve, as a wife for Adam. He gave them a beautiful garden called Eden, where he lived and walked among them. He assigned them to care for the garden and told them they could eat fruit from all the trees except one—the tree of the knowledge of good and evil. If they ate from that tree, God told Adam and Eve they would surely die.

Adam and Eve lived as God's people, in God's place, walking and delighting in God. Eden was heaven on earth, and everything was very good. You might say it was Christmas every day, for God was with them and everything was just as it should be. God commanded Adam and Eve to fill the earth with children.

As Adam and Eve walked with God and obeyed his commands, they always knew joy; they never knew fear. They could eat from the tree of life and live forever. But Adam and Eve never got to taste that eternal fruit.

Not long after creation, the evil one, Satan, entered Eden as a serpent. Soon he tempted Eve to eat from the *one* tree God had made off limits. Eve obeyed the serpent, took a bite, and disobeyed God. Then Adam followed Eve and did the same. And so, sin entered the world for the very first time. All at once, Adam and Eve were aware of their nakedness. They quickly covered themselves with leaves, to hide their shame.

Of course, God knew that Adam and Eve had sinned. He wasn't at all surprised, and he immediately went to find them.

If you recall, God had said earlier that the punishment for eating from that tree was death. So when God called to Adam and Eve, they were afraid and tried hiding from him. But it's impossible to hide from God. When he stood before them, he asked them what had happened. Adam blamed Eve and Eve blamed the serpent. Again, God wasn't surprised. He knew from eternity past—even before he created the earth—that Adam and Eve would disobey him. And so, long before time began, God planned to extend mercy through a Christmas promise: forgiveness.

God promised that a future Son would bruise (crush) the serpent's head and reverse sin's curse. While God did not explain how the future Son would accomplish this, he did provide a clue. Forgiveness required the shedding of blood. So, God killed animals, and from their hides, he made clothing to cover Adam and Eve's shame. The animals sacrificed that day were a picture of the cost of forgiveness. One day, the Lamb of God, Jesus, would die to cover the sins of God's people.

Till then, God cursed the land. Thorns would invade, making it hard for Adam to grow food. Eve would experience pain in childbirth. And God made them leave Eden, and the tree of life, forever. He posted an angel to stand guard so they could never return. Without the fruit from the tree of life, Adam and Eve would grow old and die. Their hope now rested in the Christmas promise of a future Son. But, because their children were born into sin, evil spread. Soon their children forgot about God, and by the days of Noah, people only did evil all the time.

QUESTIONS:

1. Who created the heavens and the earth?
2. What did God say would be the punishment for sin?
3. What is the Christmas promise God gave Adam and Eve?
4. How did the animal skins point to Jesus?

Answers: (1) God created the heavens and the earth out of nothing, by the power of his command. (2) The penalty for sin is death. (3) Forgiveness: One day, a future Son would be born to bruise [crush] the head of the serpent. (4) Just as the animal skins covered Adam and Eve's nakedness and shame, the blood of Christ covers our sin and shame. For by his death, we are forgiven.

INTRODUCTION

"MY EYES LONG FOR YOUR SALVATION AND FOR THE FULFILLMENT OF YOUR RIGHTEOUS PROMISE." PSALM 119:123

Promises Made explores the key Christmas promises God made to his people before the birth of Christ. I call them "Christmas" promises because God fulfilled all of them through the life, ministry, and death of Jesus, whose birth we celebrate on Christmas.

From the moment Adam and Eve sinned, God provided the promise of a Savior. Through grace, Eve would give birth to a Son. While the wicked serpent would strike his heel, the Son would crush the serpent's head, restoring Adam and Eve's relationship with God. For generations, the Son would speak as a Prophet, reign as a King, serve as a Shepherd, and be God incarnate.

Studying the Christmas promises encourages us to treasure the true meaning of Christmas; it fosters faith and joy. The prophets who foretold these promises longed to see them come to pass, but did not live to see the day of Christ's birth. We, however, are privileged to celebrate the coming of the prophesied Savior every Christmas morning.

Promises Made is designed to be started one week before Christmas. Beginning on December 18, read one chapter (four pages) each day and discuss the listed questions as a family.

After reading "The Greatest Sign of All Time" (the final story in *Promises Made*) on Christmas Eve, here is an idea for how to transition to reading *Promises Kept*. Early Christmas morning, set the book with the *Promises Kept* cover face up, on a white cloth (representing God's forgiveness). If you wish, surround it with treats and baked goods to celebrate Christmas. Your children will wake up to the wonderful surprise, and you can begin by reading "The Waiting Is Over" (the first story in *Promises Kept*). Read a new story every day for the next week.

1

THE PROMISE OF A SON

GENESIS 1–3; 6:5
ROMANS 5:12–17
HEBREWS 11:3

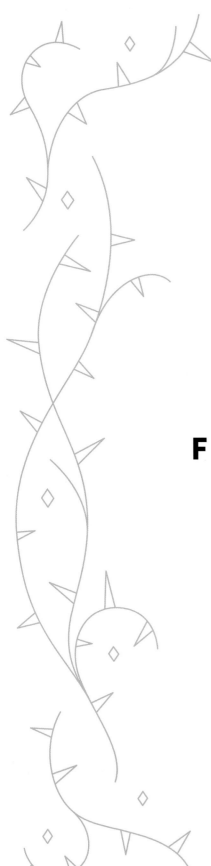

2

A PROMISE
FOR THE NATIONS

GENESIS 17:5–8; 21:5; 22:1–17
HEBREWS 11:19

A S THE OFFSPRING OF ADAM AND EVE
MULTIPLIED AND FILLED THE EARTH,
SO DID THEIR SIN. Soon they turned
against God completely. They became so evil
that God actually felt sorry that he had made
them. So, he made a plan to start over. He would
bring judgment on the entire earth through a
worldwide flood.

Thankfully, there was still one man on the earth
who loved and trusted God. His name was Noah
(Genesis 6–9). God chose to save Noah and his
family in order to continue the Christmas promise
he first gave Adam and Eve. Though the flood
destroyed the earth, God kept Noah and his family

safe in an ark. When the flood was over and the
ark reached land, God told Noah's family to fill the
earth with children again. Noah's grandchildren
would preserve the Christmas promise to raise up
a future Son to break sin's curse.

While the flood cleansed the world of evil, it
couldn't completely remove sin. It had already
spread to every descendant of Adam and Eve,
including Noah's family. Soon they wanted to
build their own way to heaven, apart from God,
by building a giant tower (Genesis 11). But instead
of destroying them, as he did in the flood, God
had mercy on his people. He confused their
languages and scattered them across the earth.

Out of all the people of all the nations, God chose Abram from Ur to carry on the Christmas promise. Even though Abram and his wife Sarai were childless and too old to bear children, God promised to give them a son. God gave Abram a new name, *Abraham*, and promised that through his descendants, kings would arise. Abraham was one hundred years old when his wife finally gave birth to their son, Isaac. The Christmas promise of a future Son and King would now come through Isaac. But first, God had to test Abraham.

When Isaac had grown, God said to Abraham, "Take your son, your only son Isaac, whom you love, and go to the land of Moriah, and offer him there as a burnt offering on one of the mountains of which I shall tell you" (Genesis 22:2). God was testing Abraham to see if he loved God more than his son.

Abraham believed in God's promise and everlasting covenant. If God allowed him to sacrifice his son, Abraham believed God would raise Isaac from the dead. So, Abraham took his son to Moriah as God directed. When they arrived, Isaac asked his father, "Where is the lamb for the offering?" Abraham answered, "God will provide the lamb."

But as Abraham took the knife to sacrifice his son, an angel of the Lord called out saying, "Do not lay your hand on the boy or do anything to him, for now I know that you fear God, seeing you have not withheld your son, your only son, from me" (Genesis 22:12). God provided a substitute sacrifice, a ram caught in the thicket, which Abraham sacrificed in place of his son. The Lord promised Abraham that because he had not withheld his only son, his descendants would be more numerous than the sand of the seashore and the stars of the sky. He promised that all the nations of the earth would be blessed through his family. The blessing of the nations is another Christmas promise.

Looking back, it is easy to see that the ram that died in Isaac's place is a picture of Jesus, whom God provided to die in our place. The call for Abraham to give up his only son is a picture of God giving up his only Son, Jesus—the far-off blessing for the nations promised to Abraham. But two thousand years would pass before Christ's birth on Christmas.

QUESTIONS:

1. How did God preserve his promise through the flood?
2. Did the flood destroy sin?
3. Why did God call Abraham to sacrifice his son Isaac as an offering to the Lord?
4. Where do we see Jesus in this story?

Answers: (1) God preserved Noah and his family on the ark. The promise of a Son would now come through the line of Noah. (2) While the flood cleansed the world of evil, it could not remove sin. (3) God tested Abraham's faith to see if he trusted God's plan. (4) The ram that died in Isaac's place points forward to Jesus, who died in our place. Abraham's willingness to sacrifice his only son, Isaac, is a picture of God giving up his only Son.

3

THE PASSOVER
AND THE PROPHET

EXODUS 10:1–2; 12:1–13
DEUTERONOMY 18:15–17

GOD KEPT HIS CHRISTMAS PROMISES THROUGH THE FAMILY OF ABRAHAM, HIS SON ISAAC, AND HIS GRANDSON JACOB, WHOM GOD RENAMED *ISRAEL*. Though Israel's sons betrayed their younger brother Joseph by selling him into slavery, God used Joseph to save his people.

God used this evil to save God's people from a great famine. Joseph rose to power and stored grain during the years of plenty, for the Lord revealed to him that a terrible famine would come. So Joseph stored away grain, which later fed and saved his people. In time, the nation of Israel multiplied and became great in Egypt. Viewing God's people as a threat, the new pharaohs that rose to power enslaved God's people.

For four hundred years, God's people suffered until God sent Moses to Pharaoh, demanding that he let God's people go. When Pharoah refused, God sent ten plagues upon Egypt before delivering his people through the Red Sea. God's Christmas promise is hidden in the tenth plague—a testimony to the children and grandchildren of Israel, that they might see God's power and believe (Exodus 10:2).

Before the arrival of the tenth plague, the death of the firstborn, God gave the families of Israel special instructions through Moses. He told them to slaughter a perfect lamb and paint its blood on the doorframes of their homes. When the angel of death came through the land and saw the blood, God said he would pass over their homes and

spare their children. All of Israel trusted in God's plan and painted their door frames with the blood. When judgment came that night, the firstborn of Israel were saved. This is a picture of how Jesus would fulfill God's promise to deliver all of God's children. Jesus lived a perfect life and took our punishment on the cross. Now his judgment passes over all who believe.

Moses's life also points to Jesus. As a baby, Pharaoh threatened Moses's life when he tried to destroy God's people. More than a thousand years later, a king named Herod tried to kill the baby Jesus. Just as God called Moses to deliver his people from slavery in Egypt, God the Father called his Son Jesus to deliver his people from slavery to sin. God also appointed Moses to serve as a mediator between him and his people. A mediator is a person who goes between two parties, helping them come to an agreement. When Israel sinned against God, Moses appealed to God on their behalf and even offered his own life in exchange for their salvation. Moses met with God and passed his law to the people. Jesus is *our* mediator. He gave his life in exchange for all those who trust in him. He now lives in heaven, praying for us. Jesus came to introduce us to his Father in heaven and provide a way for us to know God.

God called Moses as a prophet. After delivering his people from slavery in Egypt, God gave his people, through Moses, another Christmas promise. Moses said, "The LORD your God will raise up for you a prophet like me from among you, from your brothers—it is to him you shall listen . . . . And the LORD said to me . . . 'I will put my words in his mouth, and he shall speak to them all that I command him'" (Deuteronomy 18:15–18).

God promised to send a Son of Adam to crush the head of the serpent. God promised to bless the nations through Abraham's offspring, and God promised to raise up a prophet like Moses. All these promises were fulfilled in the coming of Christ on Christmas.

QUESTIONS:

1. Who did God send to deliver Israel from slavery?
2. How does the tenth plague point forward to Jesus's death on the cross?
3. In what ways did the life and ministry of Moses point forward to Jesus?

Answers: (1) God sent Moses to Egypt to deliver Israel. (2) The judgment of God passed over the homes with the lamb's blood upon their door frames. This pointed to the day when Jesus would die on the cross to cover our sins, sparing us from God's judgment. (3) Like Jesus, when he was a baby, Moses escaped the evil decree of a ruler who wanted to take his life. Moses lived as a prophet for Israel and spoke God's words to them. Moses also mediated for Israel by praying for the people, asking God to forgive them when they sinned.

4

THE REVELATION
OF A KING

EXODUS 29:45–46
1 SAMUEL 8:4–8; 15:10–12
2 SAMUEL 7:12–14

I N THE DAYS OF MOSES, GOD LED AND LIVED AMONG HIS PEOPLE IN A PILLAR OF CLOUD BY DAY AND A PILLAR OF FIRE BY NIGHT. Though he was the greatest Ruler and King, even his own people soon rejected him. This was because they longed for an earthly king—one they could see and touch. One that looked strong and mighty, like the kings of other nations. So, they told the prophet Samuel to ask God to give them a king. Though this saddened Samuel, God told him to honor their request, for through their prayer, God would fulfill another Christmas promise. God planned for the Son of Promise to take up the throne of Israel and reign forever.

Samuel obeyed the Lord and anointed Saul king over Israel. Saul began ruling well, in humility and obedience to God. But unfortunately, it did not last. One day, when God commanded Saul to destroy a people called the Amalekites, he didn't fully obey. You see, God also told Saul to destroy *everything* the Amalekites owned (they had worshiped idols). When Saul took Israel into battle against the Amalekites, they won a great victory. But instead of following the Lord's command to destroy everything, Saul allowed his soldiers to keep the Amalekite sheep and oxen. He also spared the life of the Amalekite king. And to make matters worse, Saul erected a monument to himself.

When God saw Saul's disobedience and pride, he spoke to Saul through Samuel: "You have not kept the command of the LORD your God, with which he commanded you. For then the LORD would have established your kingdom over Israel forever. But now your kingdom shall not continue. The LORD has sought out a man after his own heart, and the LORD has commanded him to be prince over his people, because you have not kept what the LORD commanded you" (1 Samuel 13:13–14).

 After Saul's disobedience, God sent Samuel to the house of Jesse to anoint one of his seven sons as the new king. At first, Samuel thought Eliab, the oldest and tallest son, should be king, but God told Samuel that he looks at people's hearts, not at their outward appearance. When the youngest son, David, was called in from tending his sheep in the fields, God directed Samuel to anoint him as the next king of Israel. David was chosen because of his love for God. And, years later when Saul died, David became the new king.

One of the great Christmas promises came to King David through the prophet Nathan. God told Nathan to tell David, "I will raise up your offspring after you, who shall come from your body, and I will establish his kingdom. He shall build a house for my name, and I will establish the throne of his kingdom forever. I will be to him a father, and he shall be to me a son" (2 Samuel 7:12b–14a). By these words, Israel learned that the Son, first promised to Adam, would rule on an eternal throne one day. The future Son of Promise came to be known as the Messiah, which means anointed one—the One God would anoint as the Everlasting King of Israel.

Even so, the Christmas promise of a future, eternal King could only be fulfilled by a sinless Son. Sadly, David also sinned against God. He murdered his soldier, Uriah, to take his wife as his own. David's son Solomon also sinned against the Lord.

One day, God would send his own Son, born into the line of David, to live a perfect, sinless life. He would offer his perfect life as a guilt offering—a sacrifice for the sins of God's people. Then, on the third day, God's Son would rise as King to rule upon the throne of David with righteousness and justice forever.

QUESTIONS:

1. Why was Samuel sad when the people of Israel asked for a king?
2. In Acts 13:22, David is described as a person after God's own heart. What does it mean to be a person after God's own heart?
3. What does the name Messiah mean, and who does it point to?

Answers: (1) Samuel was sad because he knew God was their King, but they rejected God by asking for an earthly king. (2) A person after God's own heart loves what God loves and hates what God hates. Jesus said it like this, "You shall love the Lord your God with all your heart and with all your soul and with all your mind" [Matthew 22:37]. (3) The name Messiah means anointed one. Jesus is the Messiah God promised to send.

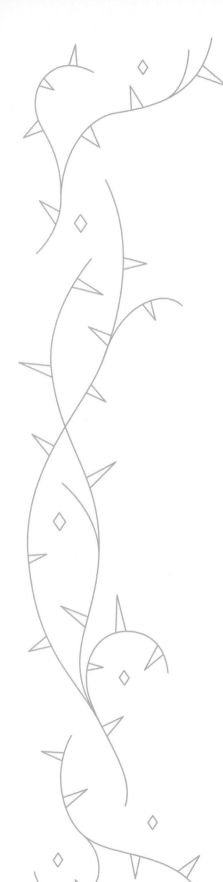

5

A SERVANT TO SUFFER

ISAIAH 37; 53; 54:5

ISAIAH SERVED AS A PROPHET SEVEN HUNDRED YEARS BEFORE JESUS WAS BORN, WHEN ISRAEL WAS DIVIDED INTO A NORTHERN KINGDOM AND A SOUTHERN KINGDOM. Isaiah frequently prophesied to God's people in the southern kingdom. He gave them more Christmas promises than any other prophet! Isaiah said that the Messiah would bring good news and set the captives free (Isaiah 61:1); the deaf would hear and the blind see (Isaiah 29:18). Isaiah comforted God's people and reminded them of his promises.

During the reign of King Hezekiah, Sennacherib, the king of Assyria, led his vast army against Jerusalem. Sennacherib mocked God and told Israel that God would not deliver them. When King Hezekiah learned of this, he tore his clothes and sent Isaiah a request for help. God spoke to Hezekiah through Isaiah. He said that the king of Assyria would not shoot a single arrow into the city and that God himself would defend the city. This was because of God's Christmas promise to David—that one of David's sons would sit upon an eternal throne. Isaiah said that Sennacherib

would return home and be slain by his own people. Isaiah, quoting God, said, "'Have you not heard that I determined it long ago? I planned from days of old what now I bring to pass'" (Isaiah 37:26). No earthly king could stop God from delivering his people through the line of David.

Just as the prophecy stated, God sent an angel into the Assyrian camp and struck down 185,000 people. Not a single arrow flew into Jerusalem. Later, when Sennacherib returned, he was killed by his own son. It was just as Isaiah had said. No other prophet foretold the future in greater detail than he did.

The book of Isaiah holds some of the most marvelous Christmas promises, but the greatest is found in chapter 53. Here, Isaiah revealed God's salvation plan—the one he did *not* allow Sennacherib to destroy. The Son of the Christmas promise, also known as God's servant, would offer his innocent life in exchange for ours—his perfect life to cover our sin.

God's servant would suffer terribly and be so brutally beaten that he could not be recognized (Isaiah 52:14). God allowed his servant to be stricken, afflicted, and punished. Isaiah prophesied, "He was pierced for our transgressions; he was crushed for our iniquities; upon him was the chastisement that brought us peace, and with his wounds we are healed. All we like sheep have gone astray; we have turned—every one— to his own way; and the LORD has laid on him the iniquity of us all" (Isaiah 53:5–6).

Isaiah predicted the Messiah would be buried in the tomb of a rich man. But Isaiah also prophesied that the grave would not hold him and he would rise again, saying God will prolong his days (Isaiah 53:10) and allow him to share in the spoils of his victory with those whom he saves (53:12). And this is what happened. Jesus, the Messiah and suffering servant, lived a perfect life, died for our sins, rose again, and returned to heaven, where he intercedes for us now. He is none other than our "Maker . . . the LORD of hosts . . . the Holy One of Israel . . . Redeemer, the God of the whole earth (Isaiah 54:5).

Isaiah also prophesied that Jesus would be called "Wonderful Counselor, Mighty God, Everlasting Father, Prince of Peace" (Isaiah 9:6b). Isaiah gave all these Christmas promises about Jesus seven hundred years before he was born.

QUESTIONS:

1. According to Isaiah, how did God plan to save us?
2. Read Isaiah 53 and list some of the prophesies about the death of God's servant.
3. What enabled God's servant to rise from the dead?
4. How could Isaiah know so much about Jesus's death seven hundred years before Jesus was born?

Answers: (1) Isaiah said the God who created us would take on our sin and die in our place. (2) Some examples: Isaiah 53 tells us that God's servant would be "despised and rejected" (v. 3), "cut off from the land of the living" (v. 8), "numbered with the transgressors" (v. 12), and "pierced for our transgressions" (v. 5). (3) God's servant lived a righteous life and did not sin (Isaiah 53:9). God raised him from the dead (Acts 2:32). (4) The Spirit of God told the prophets of the sufferings of Christ. (See 1 Peter 1:10–11.)

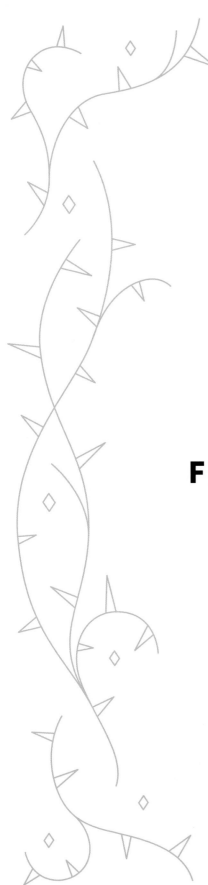

6

A SHEPHERD
FROM BETHLEHEM

EZEKIEL 34:11–15, 23–24
JEREMIAH 23:1–4
MICAH 2:12–13

ANOTHER OF GOD'S CHRISTMAS PROMISES WAS THAT THE MESSIAH WOULD BE A SHEPHERD TO HIS PEOPLE. Shepherds gather, lead, and protect their flocks. The idea of a shepherd goes all the way back to Adam's son Abel, who offered the very best of his flock to God. His generous sacrifice reminds us of God's generosity in giving his very best sacrifice, his own Son.

The Bible also mentions that Abraham and Moses were shepherds. So was David. Their job as shepherds was to protect their flocks from evil and to lead them to safety. This is a picture of how the Son of God would shepherd and protect God's children (the Father's sheep).

The prophet Ezekiel foretold that the Shepherd of the Christmas Promise would arise from the line of David (see Ezekiel 34:23). He also revealed that this Shepherd would be no ordinary man:

For thus says the Lord GOD: Behold, I, I myself will search for my sheep and will seek them out. As a shepherd seeks out his flock when he is among his sheep that have been scattered, so will I seek out my sheep, and I will rescue them from all places where they have been scattered . . . I myself will be the shepherd of my sheep, and I myself will make them lie down, declares the Lord GOD. Ezekiel 34:11–12, 15

Jesus was not only a son in the line of David, he was also the Son of God, the Promised One. John tells us that Jesus is the Shepherd who will wipe away all our tears, and the One who guides us to springs of living water (Revelation 7:17).

Ezekiel is not the only prophet to describe the Messiah as a shepherd. Jeremiah said, "I will gather the remnant of my flock out of all the countries where I have driven them, and I will bring them back to their fold, and they shall be fruitful and multiply. I will set shepherds over them who will care for them, and they shall fear no more, nor be dismayed, neither shall any be missing, declares the LORD" (Jeremiah 23:3–4).

The prophet Zechariah foretold that the Shepherd would face the sword and be struck down, a prophecy of the future sacrifice of Jesus. Zechariah wrote: "'Awake, O sword, against my shepherd, against the man who stands next to me,' declares the LORD of hosts. 'Strike the shepherd, and the sheep will be scattered'" (Zechariah 13:7).

The prophet Micah announced that the Shepherd of the Christmas promise would arise from the clan of Judah and be born in Bethlehem, the city of David:

> But you, O Bethlehem Ephrathah, who are too little to be among the clans of Judah, from you shall come forth for me one who is to be ruler in Israel, whose coming forth is from of old, from ancient days. Therefore he shall give them up until the time when she who is in labor has given birth; then the rest of his brothers shall return to the people of Israel. And he shall stand and shepherd his flock in the strength of the LORD, in the majesty of the name of the LORD his God. And they shall dwell secure, for now he shall be great to the ends of the earth. Micah 5:2–4

More than seven hundred years passed from the time of Micah's prophecy to the birth of Jesus in the city of David (Bethlehem). When the time came for the Messiah's birth, a great company of angels announced his birth—not to the kings of the earth, but to a group of shepherds on a hillside.

QUESTIONS:

1. What were some of the names of the shepherds in the Bible?
2. Why is the picture of a shepherd caring for the sheep an excellent way to describe God's care for his people?
3. Who is the shepherd that God promised to send?
4. How long did the people of Israel have to wait until the prophet Micah's Christmas promises were fulfilled?

Answers: (1) Moses, Abraham, and David were all shepherds whom God called. (2) Shepherds care for the sheep, just as God cares for his people. Shepherds know their sheep by name, just as God knows each of us. And shepherds protect the sheep, just as God protects us. (3) Jesus is the shepherd God promised to send. (4) They waited seven hundred years until Christ was born.

7

THE GREATEST SIGN
OF ALL TIME

ISAIAH 7:1–14; 9:1–7
LUKE 1:26–38

A MOST REMARKABLE CHRISTMAS PROMISE WAS GIVEN BY THE PROPHET ISAIAH TO KING AHAZ WHEN TWO ARMIES STOOD AGAINST JERUSALEM. God sent Isaiah to assure the king of the Lord's protection. Even though Ahaz was wicked, God extended mercy. When Ahaz learned of the armies ready to attack, he shook with fear (Isaiah 7:2).

Isaiah comforted Ahaz and told him the Lord would protect him and that Ahaz should ask the Lord for a sign of this salvation. Isaiah told Ahaz, "Ask a sign of the LORD your God; let it be deep as Sheol or high as heaven" (Isaiah 7:11). Even though Ahaz was a wicked king God offered to show him a sign of his salvation.

If King Ahaz had asked God as a sign to split the sun in half, God would have done it. But Ahaz was afraid. He didn't want to test God. Isaiah responded by giving Ahaz the greatest sign of all time, even greater than splitting the sun. He said, "The Lord himself will give you a sign. Behold, the virgin shall conceive and bear a son, and shall call his name Immanuel" (Isaiah 7:14). The name *Immanuel* means God with us. So the child Isaiah foretold would be both God and man.

Not only did the Lord deliver Jerusalem from the hand of their enemies, but he also gave King Ahaz the greatest sign of all time: the promise of his coming Son.

Seven hundred years later, the angel Gabriel echoed God's Christmas promise to Mary with these words:

> "Do not be afraid, Mary, for you have found favor with God. And behold, you will conceive in your womb and bear a son, and you shall call his name Jesus. He will be great and will be called the Son of the Most High. And the Lord God will give to him the throne of his father David, and he will reign over the house of Jacob forever, and of his kingdom there will be no end."
>
> And Mary [who was unmarried] said to the angel, "How will this be, since I am a virgin?"
>
> And the angel answered her, "The Holy Spirit will come upon you, and the power of the Most High will overshadow you; therefore the child to be born will be called holy—the Son of God." Luke 1:30–35

Through Mary's trust in God, the King of glory stepped off his throne and became human. Immanuel, God with us, filled the womb of a young, unmarried woman—an impossible plan made possible through God.

On the day Isaiah spoke to Ahaz, he also spoke of the child to be born, saying: "For to us a child is born, to us a son is given; and the government shall be upon his shoulder, and his name shall be called Wonderful Counselor, Mighty God, Everlasting Father, Prince of Peace. Of the increase of his government and of peace there will be no end, on the throne of David and over his kingdom, to establish it and to uphold it with justice and with righteousness from this time forth and forevermore. The zeal of the LORD of hosts will do this" (Isaiah 9:6–7).

Our excitement in waiting for Christmas is just a tiny glimpse into how God's people waited seven hundred years for the fulfillment of God's promised Son.

QUESTIONS:

1. What was the greatest sign of all time?
2. How is the promise Gabriel gave Mary, the same as the sign spoken to Ahaz?
3. When was the greatest sign of all time fulfilled?

Answers: (1) The greatest sign of all time was that a virgin would give birth to the divine Son of God. (2) The sign spoken to Ahaz had two parts. First, a virgin (Mary) would conceive a child and give birth. Second, the baby would be called Immanuel, which means God with us. The angel told Mary her son would be the Son of the Most High—God's Son. (3) The greatest sign of all time was fulfilled when Mary gave birth to Jesus on Christmas.

NOT THE END OF THE STORY
FLIP BOOK OVER TO READ *PROMISES KEPT*

the angels reminded the disciples that he would return, saying, "This Jesus, who was taken up from you into heaven, will come in the same way as you saw him go into heaven" (Acts 1:11b). One day the King of Kings will return.

Today, we are still waiting for King Jesus's return in the clouds. His return will fulfill the last of the Christmas promises: he will have the final victory over sin and death. God gave a vision of that victory to the apostle John, who wrote,

> Then I saw heaven opened, and behold, a white horse! The one sitting on it is called Faithful and True, and in righteousness he judges and makes war. His eyes are like a flame of fire, and on his head are many diadems, and he has a name written that no one knows but himself. He is clothed in a robe dipped in blood, and the name by which he is called is The Word of God. And the armies of heaven, arrayed in fine linen, white and pure, were following him on white horses. From his mouth comes a sharp sword with which to strike down the nations, and he will rule them with a rod of iron. He will tread the winepress of the fury of the wrath of God the Almighty. On his robe and on his thigh he has a name written, King of kings and Lord of lords. Revelation 19:11–16

At the end of his vision, John recorded the last promise of Jesus: "I am coming soon. Blessed is the one who keeps the words of the prophecy of this book" (Revelation 22:7).

Each year on December 25th, we celebrate the advent, or coming, of Jesus. Now, as we begin another new year, we await the second advent—the return of King Jesus. At that time, he will fulfill his final promise in defeating death and making all things new. He will then gather his people from every tribe and nation, and together, we will all worship our King. We will live in a new garden and eat from the tree of life and live forever.

QUESTIONS:

1. What is the promise that is yet to be fulfilled?
2. Who will be gathered around the throne of Jesus after his return?
3. How has God encouraged your heart though this study?

Answers: (1) The final promise is Christ's return to earth. He will defeat death and evil and make all things new. (2) There will be people from every nation gathered around the throne, all worshiping Jesus, their Savior. This will fulfill God's promise to Abraham. (3) Answers will vary.

JESUS FULFILLED THE LONG-AWAITED PROPHECY OF A COMING KING. Shortly after his birth, wise men from the east followed a star to Bethlehem, believing it marked the birth of the King of promise. The wise men asked King Herod, "Where is he who has been born king of the Jews? For we saw his star when it rose and have come to worship him" (Matthew 2:2). Years later, when Jesus rode into Jerusalem on a donkey, the people shouted, "Blessed is the King who comes in the name of the Lord" (Luke 19:38a). They believed Jesus was the fulfillment of Zechariah's prophecy: "Behold, your king is coming to you; righteous and having salvation is he, humble and mounted on a donkey" (Zechariah 9:9b).

After Jesus's arrest, the chief priest asked him if he was the Messiah, to which he replied, "I am, and you will see the Son of Man seated at the right hand of Power, and coming with the clouds of heaven" (Mark 14:62). By these words, Jesus claimed the throne of David. When questioned by Pilate, Jesus admitted he was a king—not an earthly king over an earthly kingdom, but a heavenly king (John 18:36). Because of this, Pilate set a sign on Jesus's cross that read: "Jesus of Nazareth, the King of the Jews" (John 19:19b).

In Hebrews, we read, "But when Christ had offered for all time a single sacrifice for sins, he sat down at the right hand of God" (10:12). When Jesus ascended to heaven and sat on the throne,

7

THE RETURN OF THE KING

ZECHARIAH 9:9
JOHN 18:33–37
REVELATION 7:9–12;
21:22–27; 22:6–21

QUESTIONS:

1. How does God plan to bless the nations now?
2. What Christmas promises did Peter say were fulfilled through the life of Jesus?
3. Now that Jesus has risen, what must we do to be saved from our sin?

Answers: (1) His charge to the disciples extends to us today: to share his good news with the world. (2) Peter said that Jesus was a prophet like Moses (Acts 3:21–22), the servant who would give his life for the sins of God's people (v. 13), and the promised blessing for the nations (v. 25). (3) We must repent, turn from our sins, and believe in Jesus's perfect life, love, and sacrifice for us.

Though Peter had earlier denied knowing Jesus, he stood before crowds with great courage, proclaiming the gospel. He told them that Jesus, whom they crucified, was the Messiah, the one who fulfilled the Christmas promises given to David to raise up an eternal King (Acts 2:30). He announced that God raised Jesus from the dead, and that the disciples were his witnesses.

The people gathered for the feast were convicted by Peter's message and asked, "What shall we do?" (Acts 2:37). Peter told them to repent, which means to turn away from their sins. He then told them to be baptized. About three thousand people believed and were baptized that day.

These new believers became the first church. They all shared their possessions to help those in need. Day by day, they went to the temple, ate meals together in their homes, and spent time in prayer and worship. The apostles performed many signs and wonders. As people witnessed this, God daily added to their number those who believed (Acts 2:46–47).

One day, when Peter and John went to the temple to pray, they met a man who was lame from birth. The man called out, asking for money. Peter replied, "I have no silver and gold, but what I do have I give to you. In the name of Jesus Christ of Nazareth, rise up and walk!" (Acts 3:6). As Peter took the man by the hand, he rose to his feet and began to walk. Then he went away leaping and praising God.

The people who saw this were amazed. They thought Peter and John were miracle workers. Peter explained that it was by faith in Jesus that the lame man was able to walk. Then Peter shared the gospel and how Jesus fulfilled all the Christmas promises. He explained that Jesus was the foretold Prophet like Moses, and Jesus fulfilled God's promise to Abraham to bless all the families on earth. Peter challenged those in the crowd to turn from their sins and believe in Jesus, whom God had raised from the dead. The people listened carefully, and hundreds believed in Jesus. But the religious leaders grew angry.

Soon the leaders arrested Peter and John and held them in custody, commanding them to stop sharing about Jesus. Peter and John said that they must obey God. The religious leaders couldn't deny the fact that the lame man now walked; after all, there were hundreds of witnesses! So, after keeping them in jail overnight, they released them. Peter and John joined the other disciples in sharing God's good news with all who would listen. They warned them to turn from their sin for one day King Jesus would return to judge the earth and destroy death forever.

I N THE DAYS FOLLOWING JESUS'S RESURRECTION, HE TAUGHT HIS disciples how the Christmas promises in Scripture were fulfilled through his life, death, and resurrection (Luke 24:27). He was the promised Son of Adam, the Blessing for the Nations, and the Prophet like Moses. Like Moses, Jesus taught people about God, prayed for the people of God, and prophesied (about the future outpouring of the Holy Spirit).

Before he returned to his Father in heaven, Jesus commissioned the disciples to proclaim this gospel message to all people. But first, Jesus told them to wait for the Holy Spirit, saying, "You will receive power when the Holy Spirit has come upon you, and you will be my witnesses in Jerusalem and in all Judea and Samaria, and to the end of the earth" (Acts 1:8). Ten days later, on the feast of Pentecost, the Spirit of God came upon the disciples and filled them with boldness.

6

A PROPHET
LIKE MOSES

JOHN 14:12–14
ACTS 2:22–41

With the words, "It is finished," Jesus declared his mission complete. As he gave his final breath, his enemies celebrated. But soon, they would discover that death could not hold the sinless Son of the Christmas promise. The thorns of Adam's curse, pressed upon Jesus's head by the Roman soldiers, became his victory crown.

After Jesus died, Roman soldiers pierced his side to make sure he was dead. This fulfilled Simeon's prophecy to Mary. Then, Joseph of Arimathea, a wealthy man, asked Pilate for permission to bury Jesus's body. Joseph laid Jesus in his own tomb, fulfilling Isaiah's prophecy that he would be laid in the tomb of a rich man (Isaiah 53:9).

Roman soldiers were charged to seal the tomb and guard it. But not even death itself could hold Jesus in the grave. Death was the punishment for sin, and Jesus had never sinned. He had lived a perfect, sinless life. He was completely innocent. And because he was conceived of the Holy Spirit, the sin of Adam did not pass on to him. Therefore, as David foretold, the Father did not abandon his Son to the grave or allow him to see decay (Psalm 16:10). On the third day, just as he promised (Matthew 17:23), Jesus rose from the grave in victory.

Matthew wrote: "There was a great earthquake, for an angel of the Lord descended from heaven and came and rolled back the stone and sat on it. His appearance was like lightning, and his clothing white as snow. And for fear of him the guards trembled and became like dead men. But the angel said to the women, 'Do not be afraid, for I know that you seek Jesus who was crucified. He is not here, for he has risen, as he said'" (Matthew 28:2–6).

The Christmas promise of a future Son who would come to crush the head of the serpent was fulfilled through the resurrection. In the days that followed, Jesus appeared to the disciples and to more than five hundred people, proving his resurrection and victory over death. Before he returned to heaven, Jesus commissioned his disciples to tell the whole world that everyone who turns from their sin and believes in Jesus will be saved.

QUESTIONS:

1. How can we be sure that Jesus's death was part of God's plan?
2. Why was Jesus not held by the grave?
3. How did Jesus prove that he rose from the dead?

Answers: (1) The prophets foretold it, Jesus predicted it, and the Bible affirms it. (See Acts 2:23.) (2) The punishment for sin was death, but Jesus never sinned. Therefore, death had no authority over him, and he was able to take up his life and rise from the dead. (3) Jesus appeared to his disciples and to over five hundred witnesses.

WHILE THE RELIGIOUS RULERS PLOTTED SECRETLY TO KILL JESUS, GOD PLANNED TO FULFILL HIS PROMISE TO ADAM AND EVE. God knew the religious rulers would send spies to trap his Son. He knew Judas would betray Jesus for thirty pieces of silver. He knew that the priests would bring false witnesses and condemn Jesus to death. And he knew the Romans would flog Jesus and crucify him alongside other criminals (Isaiah 53:12). God knew it all and foretold it long ago through his prophets.

Isaiah prophesied that Jesus would be rejected (Isaiah 53:3) and that God's servant would suffer. David said his hands and feet would be pierced, and that the soldiers would cast lots for his garments (Psalm 22:16, 18). David wrote the betrayer would be a close friend and share a meal with Jesus (Psalm 41:9). The prophet Zechariah foretold the price of his betrayal would be thirty pieces of silver, and that Judas would return the blood money, casting it on the floor of the temple (Zechariah 11:12, 13).

While the great serpent lurked behind these evil deeds and even entered Judas at the time of the betrayal, every detail unfolded "according to the definite plan and foreknowledge of God" (Acts 2:23). Beyond the suffering of the cross imposed by men, God the Father poured out the judgment for our sin upon Jesus. Isaiah said, "The LORD has laid on him the iniquity of us all" (Isaiah 53:6b). During Jesus's suffering on the cross, he prayed Psalm 22:1a, "My God, my God, why have you forsaken me?"

5

ADAM'S PROMISE
FULFILLED

MATTHEW 26:14–16
LUKE 20:20; 23:27; 28:1–10
ACTS 2:23

With these words, Jesus compared his mission to save sinners with the work of a shepherd searching for lost sheep.

One day, after healing a man who was blind from birth, Jesus declared:

> I am the good shepherd. The good shepherd lays down his life for the sheep. He who is a hired hand and not a shepherd, who does not own the sheep, sees the wolf coming and leaves the sheep and flees, and the wolf snatches them and scatters them. He flees because he is a hired hand and cares nothing for the sheep. I am the good shepherd. I know my own and my own know me, just as the Father knows me and I know the Father; and I lay down my life for the sheep. John 10:11–15

This teaching was a fulfillment of the Christmas promises, but it wasn't received well by everyone. There were some who did not believe that Jesus was the Messiah. Though they couldn't deny his power in healing the sick, some people thought Jesus was crazy. Others thought he was demon-possessed. When Jesus raised Lazarus from the dead, the religious rulers grew jealous. They were terrified of losing their own power. They cared more for themselves than for God's people. Fueled by their jealousy and fearful of Rome, they planned to kill Jesus (John 11:48, 53).

Jesus was not surprised by this turn of events. Quoting the prophet Zechariah, Jesus warned his disciples the night of his arrest, "You will all fall away because of me this night. For it is written, 'I will strike the shepherd, and the sheep of the flock will be scattered'" (Matthew 26:31). Jesus knew that he came to die for the sheep of Israel saying, "For this reason the Father loves me, because I lay down my life that I may take it up again. No one takes it from me, but I lay it down of my own accord. I have authority to lay it down, and I have authority to take it up again. This charge I have received from my Father" (John 10:17–18).

QUESTIONS:

1. Who is the Good Shepherd in the parable?
2. Who are the two groups of sheep that Jesus came to rescue?
3. How did the religious leaders feel about Jesus and his following?
4. How are we like lost sheep?

Answers: (1) Jesus is the Good Shepherd (2) The sheep of the fold were the people of Israel, and those outside the fold were his children from other nations. Jesus taught that he would bring those outside, into the fold (Israel) and make them one flock. (3) The religious leaders were jealous of the crowds following Jesus; they were afraid they would lose their power, so they planned to kill Jesus. (4) We are all sinners who are separated from God. We need Jesus to rescue us and welcome us into his flock.

AS JESUS TRAVELED THROUGHOUT THE LAND OF JUDEA, he proclaimed the good news of the gospel. He announced that he was the Shepherd the prophets promised would come. Matthew records that when Jesus saw the crowds of people, he had compassion on them, for he saw that they were helpless, like sheep without a shepherd (Matthew 9:36). This is what the prophet Zechariah had said about God's people: they "wander like sheep; they are afflicted for lack of a shepherd" (Zechariah 10:2b).

Many of the prophets foretold of God's Shepherd. Isaiah wrote, "He will tend his flock like a shepherd; he will gather the lambs in his arms" (Isaiah 40:11a). Jeremiah said, "Hear the word of the LORD, O nations . . . 'He who scattered Israel will gather him, and will keep him as a shepherd keeps his flock'" (Jeremiah 31:10). Jesus was the

Shepherd of these promises. He also fulfilled the prophecy of Ezekiel, who said, the Messiah would come as a shepherd to rescue God's sheep from all the places they were scattered (Ezekiel 34:12b).

Read how Jesus described his own ministry:

"What man of you, having a hundred sheep, if he has lost one of them, does not leave the ninety-nine in the open country, and go after the one that is lost, until he finds it? And when he has found it, he lays it on his shoulders, rejoicing. And when he comes home, he calls together his friends and his neighbors, saying to them, 'Rejoice with me, for I have found my sheep that was lost.' Just so, I tell you, there will be more joy in heaven over one sinner who repents than over ninety-nine righteous persons who need no repentance." Luke 15:4–7

4

THE GOOD SHEPHERD

MATTHEW 26:31
LUKE 15:4–7
JOHN 10:1–18; 11:45–53

When Jesus shared that God now welcomed Gentiles into his kingdom (because the Israelites had rejected God's message), the people grew angry. They chased Jesus out of the synagogue and out of Nazareth. They marched him right up to the edge of a cliff and tried to push him off—to his death! But since it was not yet time for Jesus to die, he slipped away through the crowd.

After leaving Nazareth, Jesus went to teach at the synagogue in Capernaum. As he began speaking, a demon-possessed man started to shout, "What have you to do with us, Jesus of Nazareth? Have you come to destroy us? I know who you are—the Holy One of God" (Luke 4:34). The demon knew Jesus was the Messiah whom Isaiah promised would come. There, in front of the crowd, Jesus rebuked the demon and ordered him to be silent and come out of the man. The demon obeyed and left the man unharmed. When the people witnessed Jesus's authority over the demon, they were amazed. Word spread throughout the land.

From the synagogue, Jesus went to Simon's house, where he healed his mother-in-law, who lay sick in bed with a fever. By sunset, word again spread, and people with all kinds of sicknesses came to Jesus for healing. He miraculously healed them all!

When another demon-possessed person called Jesus the Son of God, he rebuked the demon and forbade him to speak. Jesus proved he was the One Isaiah said would come by setting the captives free. Jesus fulfilled the Scriptures in delivering people from demons, healing the sick, and opening the eyes of the blind.

The next day, when Jesus went to leave Capernaum, the people asked him to stay. He replied, "I must preach the good news of the kingdom of God to the other towns as well; for I was sent for this purpose" (Luke 4:43). After seven hundred years, God kept his Christmas promise to send the Messiah to proclaim good news to the poor, set the captives free, and give sight to the blind (Isaiah 42:7; 61:1).

QUESTIONS:

1. How did Jesus fulfill God's promises given through the prophet Isaiah?
2. What did the demons reveal about the identity of Jesus?
3. Why did the people of Nazareth get so angry with Jesus?

Answers: (1) Isaiah said the Messiah would bring good news, set the captives free, and give sight to the blind. Jesus did all of these things. (2) The demons called Jesus the Holy One of God and the Son of God. (3) Jesus told them God's salvation through him would be rejected by Israel and given to the Gentiles. The people of Israel hated the Gentiles, so they also hated Jesus for what he said.

A S JESUS GREW OLDER, HE BEGAN HIS MINISTRY. Satan tried to tempt Jesus, but Jesus did not fall for his lies. Now it was time for Jesus to announce that he was the Christmas Promise the prophet Isaiah had foretold would come.

One day, as was Jesus's custom, he went to preach in the synagogue in Nazareth. The attendant handed Jesus the scroll of Isaiah, and Jesus found the place where it read: "The Spirit of the Lord is upon me, because he has anointed me to proclaim good news to the poor. He has sent me to proclaim liberty to the captives and recovering of sight to the blind, to set at liberty those who are oppressed, to proclaim the year of the Lord's favor" (Luke 4:18–19 [Isaiah 61:1–2]).

Jesus then said, "Today this Scripture has been fulfilled in your hearing" (v. 21). With those words, Jesus claimed that he was the Messiah, the One Isaiah promised would come.

At first, the people marveled at Jesus's words. After all, they had watched him grow up in Nazareth. They were his neighbors; he was Joseph's son. But then things took a terrible turn.

3

FREEDOM FOR
THE CAPTIVES

ISAIAH 29:18
LUKE 4:16–41

baptizing them in the name of the Father and of the Son and of the Holy Spirit, teaching them to observe all that I have commanded you" (Matthew 28:19–20). One day in heaven, people from every nation will gather around the throne of God to worship and praise the Lamb who was slain (Revelation 7:9–10).

That day, there was a woman named Anna who often visited the temple to fast and pray. When she saw Jesus, she recognized him as the long-awaited Savior. She praised God and shared the good news with everyone she could—that God had kept his promises and the day of Israel's redemption had come (Luke 2:36–38)!

QUESTIONS:

1. Why did Mary and Joseph take Jesus to the temple?
2. How did God keep his promise to bless the nations through Jesus?
3. What did Simeon mean when he said a sword would pierce Mary's soul?
4. What did Jesus tell his disciples to do, to carry on his mission?

Answers: (1) The law of Moses required that they offer a sacrifice to redeem their son before God. (2) Jesus died for the sins of all people, and one day, people from every nation will gather around his throne in praise. (3) Jesus's mother, Mary, was present at the cross the day Jesus died. The soldiers pierced Jesus's side with a sword. Sadness pierced Mary's soul as she watched her son die. (4) Jesus told his disciples to take the gospel to all the nations and teach them everything he commanded them.

Simeon's prayer confirmed that God would keep his promise to Abraham to bless the nations. Through Jesus, the door of salvation was now open to all Gentiles. The word *Gentile* refers to non-Jewish people. They, too, were now welcomed into God's kingdom. Through Jesus, God would keep his promise to Abraham that the people of all nations would be blessed through one of his far-off grandsons. After Simeon blessed Jesus, he gave a sober, prophetic word to Mary

and Joseph. He told them that Jesus's ministry would divide Israel, and there would be those who would oppose Jesus. In the end, a sword would pierce their son—and his mother. This pointed to Jesus's death on the cross and Mary's grief in seeing her son die (Luke 2:34–35).

After his death and resurrection, Jesus kept God's promise to Abraham through these words: "Go therefore and make disciples of all nations,

I N THE DAYS OF MOSES, GOD SENT TEN PLAGUES AGAINST EGYPT TO CONVINCE PHARAOH TO LET GOD'S PEOPLE GO. After nine plagues had all but destroyed Egypt, Pharaoh still refused. So, God brought one final plague, the death of the firstborn, to all the land. God spared the firstborn of the Israelites, who painted the blood of a lamb on their doorframes. He then declared, "the first . . . belongs to me" (Exodus 13:2 NIV).

From that day onward, God commanded Israel to celebrate the Passover every year. He also required that every firstborn son of Israel be redeemed by offering a sacrifice to God. The events of that first Passover pointed forward to Jesus, the Lamb of God. Jesus shed his blood so that God's judgment would *pass over* all those who put their faith in him. The feast of the Passover and the redeeming of the firstborn became important traditions that continued for more than a thousand years, up to the birth of Christ.

When it was time for Jesus to be redeemed, Mary and Joseph brought him to the temple, along with an offering for the sacrifice. According to the law of Moses, forty days had passed, and they, too, were required to offer a sacrifice to God for their firstborn son. Even as an infant, Jesus, with the help of his parents, kept the law perfectly.

Now there was an elderly man named Simeon who, led by the Spirit, came into the temple that day. God had told him that he would not die until he saw the fulfillment of God's Christmas promise to send the Messiah. When Simeon saw Mary and Joseph with Jesus, the Holy Spirit signaled that Jesus was the One he had been waiting for. So, Simeon walked over, took the baby Jesus into his arms, and blessed him.

As Simeon held Jesus in his arms, he prayed, "Lord, now you are letting your servant depart in peace, according to your word; for my eyes have seen your salvation that you have prepared in the presence of all peoples, a light for revelation to the Gentiles, and for glory to your people Israel" (Luke 2:29–32).

2

A BLESSING FOR THE NATIONS

EXODUS 13:11–16
MATTHEW 28:16–20
LUKE 2:22–38

God kept his promise to bring forth a son in the line of David, from the family of Abraham, a son of Adam, to break the curse of sin. Mary and Joseph were the only ones who knew of the birth of this Christmas promise, but that would soon change.

On a starry night, a group of shepherds watched over their flocks. God chose these shepherds to be the first to hear the fulfillment of his promise with the birth of his son. One of the prophecies God fulfilled was to raise up a shepherd to lead his people. God, through the prophet Ezekiel had said: "I will set up over them one shepherd, my servant David, and he shall feed them . . . and be their shepherd. And I, the LORD, will be their God, and my servant David shall be prince among them" (Ezekiel 34:23–24). Since Ezekiel prophesied more than 300 years after King David's death, we know Ezekiel is pointing forward to Jesus. The baby Jesus born in a manger would grow up to fulfill this promise.

What had seemed like an ordinary night of watching the sheep, became extraordinary. The glory of the Lord burst forth, and an angel appeared to the shepherds. They trembled as they heard the announcement: "Fear not, for behold, I bring you good news of great joy that will be for all the people. For unto you is born this day in the city of David a Savior, who is Christ the Lord. And this will be a sign for you: you will find a baby wrapped in swaddling cloths and lying in a manger" (Luke 2:10–12).

God's angel army appeared in the sky and burst into praise, saying, "Glory to God in the highest, and on earth peace among those with whom he is pleased!" (Luke 2:14). The shepherds left at once to see the fulfillment of the Christmas promise, and they found the child just as the angel had said. As the shepherds told Mary and Joseph all that had happened, Mary treasured their words in her heart.

Soon the shepherds returned to their flocks, glorifying and praising God, for the Lord had kept his promise; Christmas had come at last!

QUESTIONS:

1. According to the angel, what would Jesus do when he grew up?
2. What sign did the angel give the shepherds to help them find the right child?
3. What does the name Immanuel mean, and what does it tell us about Jesus?
4. Read through Jesus's family tree in Matthew 1:2–16 and Luke 3:23–38. How does his family line show that Jesus is the Son of the promise?

Answers: (1) The angel said that Jesus would save his people from their sins. (2) The angel told the shepherds they would find the baby wrapped in swaddling cloths and lying in a manger. (3) Immanuel means God with us, which tells us that Jesus was born a human child, but he was also God. (4) Jesus is a far-off grandson of Adam, Abraham, and David, and is therefore qualified to fulfill God's promises.

GENERATIONS HAD PASSED SINCE THE DREADFUL DAY WHEN EVE ATE THE FORBIDDEN FRUIT. On that day, God had promised to send a Son to crush the head of the serpent. When an angel announced to Mary that she would give birth to the Messiah, hope was born.

However, when Joseph learned that his fiancée, Mary, was pregnant, he was troubled. He decided to secretly end their engagement. Thankfully, an angel appeared to him in a dream and said, "Do not fear to take Mary as your wife, for that which is conceived in her is from the Holy Spirit. She will bear a son, and you shall call his name Jesus, for he will save his people from their sins" (Matthew 1:20b–21).

The angel's words echoed the Christmas promise given long before to King Ahaz: "'Behold, the virgin shall conceive and bear a son, and they shall call his name Immanuel' (which means, God with us)" (v. 23). By faith, Joseph chose to trust this message from God and remained betrothed to Mary.

It wasn't long before Caesar Augustus, the ruler of Rome, called for a census to count all the people of the land. Because Joseph was a son in the line of David, he was required to travel to the city of David, also known as Bethlehem. Mary joined him.

By the time they arrived, there was no place for Joseph and Mary to stay. Their only option was a stable. And it was in the stable—filled with dirt, animals, and hay—where Mary gave birth to Jesus. She wrapped him in swaddling cloths and laid him in a manger.

1

THE WAITING
IS OVER

EZEKIEL 34:23
MATTHEW 1:20–25
LUKE 2:1–21

INTRODUCTION

Promises Kept explores how God fulfilled his long-awaited Christmas promises. Though Israel yearned for an earthly king to free them from Rome's oppression, the last thing they considered was redemption through a baby born in a stable. Apart from the announcement of the angels, who would have guessed that this child from Bethlehem would one day crush the serpent?

Even after Jesus rose from the dead, the disciples were slow to believe. On the afternoon of his resurrection, Jesus walked along the road with two of his disciples. Hearing their unbelief, he said, "'How foolish you are, and how slow to believe all that the prophets have spoken! Did not the Messiah have to suffer these things and then enter his glory?'" (Luke 24:25–26 NIV). Then Jesus revealed how he was the fulfillment of all the Christmas promises. "Beginning with Moses and all the Prophets, he explained to them what was said in all the Scriptures concerning himself" (v. 27 NIV). *Promises Kept* walks you through this journey.

On Christmas morning, read one story and share a special treat or baked good together to celebrate Christ's birth. Then read one story a day for the week that follows. As you read, you are invited to be changed just like the people in the stories.

CONTENTS

PROMISES MADE

PROMISES KEPT

A FAMILY DEVOTIONAL
FOR CHRISTMAS

MARTY MACHOWSKI

ILLUSTRATED BY PHIL SCHORR

New
Growth
Press

TRUTHFORLIFE®

THE BIBLE-TEACHING MINISTRY OF **ALISTAIR BEGG**

The mission of Truth For Life is to teach the Bible with clarity and relevance so that unbelievers will be converted, believers will be established, and local churches will be strengthened.

Daily Program

Each day, Truth For Life distributes the Bible teaching of Alistair Begg across the U.S. and in several locations outside of the U.S. through 2,000 radio outlets. To find a radio station near you, visit **truthforlife.org/stationfinder**.

Free Teaching

The daily program, and Truth For Life's entire teaching library of over 3,000 Bible-teaching messages, can be accessed for free online at **truthforlife.org** and through Truth For Life's mobile app, which can be download for free from your app store.

At-Cost Resources

Books and audio studies from Alistair Begg are available for purchase at cost, with no markup. Visit **truthforlife.org/store**.

Where to Begin?

If you're new to Truth For Life and would like to know where to begin listening and learning, find starting point suggestions at **truthforlife.org/firststep**. For a full list of ways to connect with Truth For Life, visit **truthforlife.org/subscribe**.

Contact Truth For Life

P.O. Box 398000 Cleveland, Ohio 44139
phone 1 (888) 588-7884   **email** letters@truthforlife.org   **truthforlife.org**